Dear Parents,

Congratulations for choosing a fun and entertaining way to help your child learn to interact with others in pleasing, socially acceptable ways!

Children have the ability to be good, and they are often eager to please. However, they often don't understand their own egocentric or self-centered behavior. This self-centeredness often leads to misbehavior, and the misbehavior often leads to negative responses from others. All too soon, your child can be caught in a destructive cycle of negative action and reaction.

The purpose of the HELP ME BE GOOD books is to help your child break the cycle of negative action and reaction. Your child will learn how to replace misbehavior with acceptable behavior. Each HELP ME BE GOOD book is designed to do the following in an enjoyable way:

1. Define a misbehavior
2. Explain the cause of the misbehavior
3. Discuss the negative effects of the misbehavior
4. Offer suggestions for replacing the misbehavior with acceptable behavior

While it is effective to read the individual HELP ME BE GOOD books when a need arises, the series was designed to follow the normal development of young children. Consequently, presenting the books to your child in the order in which they are listed on the back cover of this book also works well.

As you and your child read the HELP ME BE GOOD books, your child will develop good behavior that will help build positive self-esteem and healthy relationships. Reading the books will also help to create a more friendly, happy atmosphere in your home. Thank you for allowing me to be a part of this exciting endeavor!

Sincerely,

Joy Berry

Joy Berry

Copyright© Joy Berry, 2022
Originally Published, 2008

All rights are reserved.

No part of this book can be duplicated or used without the prior written permission of the copyright owner, except for the use of brief quotations from the book.

For inquiries or permission requests contact the publisher.

Published by Joy Berry Enterprises
www.joyberryenterprises.com

A Help Me Be Good Book About

Snooping

Written By Joy Berry
Illustrated By Bartholomew

Copyright © 2008 by Joy Berry

This book is about Sam and his sister Maggie.

Reading about Sam and Maggie can help you understand and deal with **snooping.**

You are snooping when you secretly look through other people's things.

You are snooping when you secretly try to find out things about other people.

Snooping is being nosy in a sneaky, meddlesome way.

No one likes it when someone snoops.

It is important to treat others the way you want to be treated.

If you do not want others to snoop, you must not snoop.

It is important to *respect other people*. Do not secretly listen in when others are talking together.

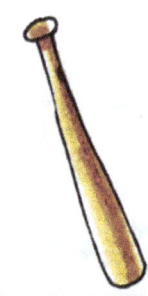

Do not secretly listen in when someone is talking on the telephone.

Do not watch other people without their knowing it.

Do not pry into another person's business. Do not try to learn things about others that they might not want you to know.

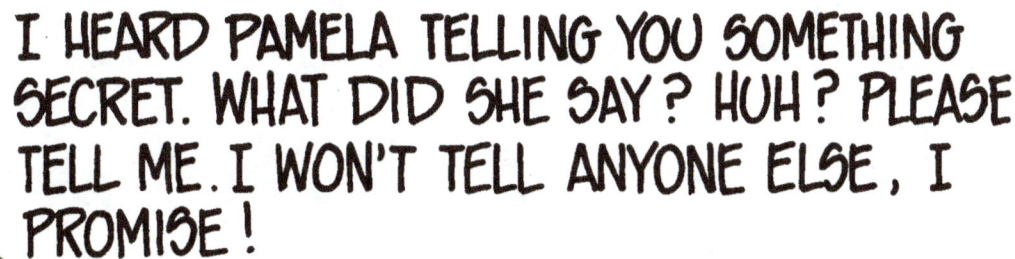

It is important to *respect other people's property*. Do not look in the windows or doors of people's houses without their knowing it.

Do not go into other people's homes unless you have permission. Do not go into a room in another person's home unless you have permission.

If a door is closed, knock on it and wait to be invited before you go in.

Do not look through another person's dresser drawers, cupboards, or closets unless you have permission.

Do not read things that belong to another person unless you have permission.

It is important *to respect other people's privacy.* People might have some thoughts and feelings they want to keep to themselves.

Do not try to make people share the thoughts and feelings they do not want to share.

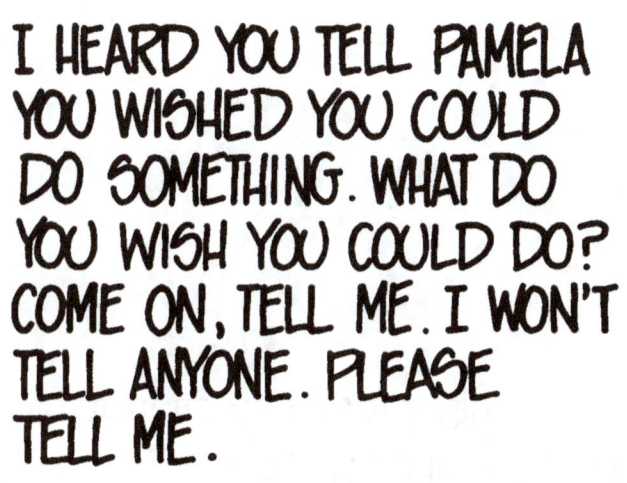

If you snoop, others might feel they cannot depend on you. They might feel they cannot trust you.

Snooping can be harmful to you and others. It is not good for you or for the people around you.

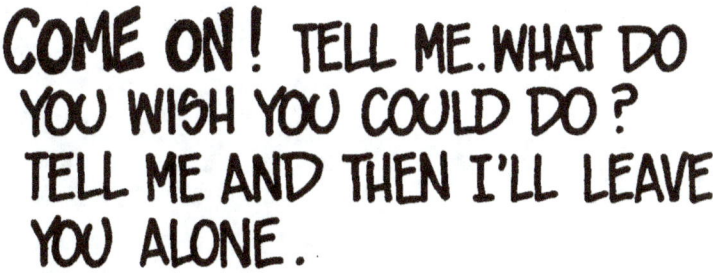

It is important to treat other people the way you want to be treated.

If you do not want other people to snoop, you must not snoop.

Snooping Song Lyrics
Music & Lyrics by Joy Berry, Lisa Petrides & Rita Abrams

It's Snooping

Going through a person's things
When they don't want you to,
That's not good to do,
Because it's snooping.

You need to respect people
And their privacy too.
Here is some advice
On what to do:
You need to treat others
Like you want them to treat you.

Listening to conversations
That aren't meant for you,
That's not good to do,
Because it's snooping.

You need to respect people
And their privacy too.
Here is some advice
On what to do:
You need to treat others
Like you want them to treat you.

Sneaking into a room
When the door is closed,
That's not good to do,
Because it's snooping.

You need to respect people
And their privacy too.
Here is some advice
On what to do:
You need to treat others
Like you want them to treat you.

Spying on other people
When they don't know you're there,
That's not good to do,
Because it's snooping.

You need to respect people
And their privacy too.
Here is some advice
On what to do:
You need to treat others
Like you want them to treat you.

Going through a person's things
When they don't want you to,
That's not good to do,
Because it's snooping.

That's not good to do,
Because it's snooping.

Snooping

I wonder what they are
Talking about,
Wonder why they are
Leaving me out.
If I listen in they'll
Never find out,
And then I will know their secret.

I don't believe it.
He's listening in.
This is our business.
It's not for him.
How can I trust him
Ever again?
I can't have a friend who's a snooper.

Everybody has to have
The right to decide
When to share their thoughts,
And when to keep them inside.
I guess I was wrong.
I guess I shouldn't have pried.
Everybody deserves their privacy.
I'm sorry.

(Part A)
I wonder what they are
Talking about,
Wonder why they are
Leaving me out.
If I listen in they'll
Never find out,
And then I will know their secret.

(Part B)
Look at the change
That's come over him.
He knows it's not right
To listen in.
Now I can trust him.
Now he's my friend.
Now he'll never be a snooper.

(Part A and B simultaneously)

Everybody has to have
The right to decide.
When to share their thoughts,
And when to keep them inside.
I don't want to listen,
And I don't want to spy.
A snooper's something that I don't want to be.

'Cause everyone deserves their privacy.

Yee!

Visit us on the web at www.joyberryenterprises.com!

www.ingramcontent.com/pod-product-compliance
Lightning Source LLC
Chambersburg PA
CBHW081411070526
44583CB00020B/2761